CAMPUS TENSIONS: ANALYSIS AND RECOMMENDATIONS

Report of the Special Committee on Campus Tensions
SOL M. LINOWITZ, Chairman

The views expressed in this Report
are those of the
Special Committee on Campus Tensions,
which bears sole responsibility for its contents.
The Report was made possible by a grant from the
Mary Reynolds Babcock Foundation
of Winston-Salem, North Carolina.

Second Impression, July 1970
Third Impression, December 1970

CONTENTS

ACKNOWLEDGMENTS. *The Committee gratefully acknowledges the assistance of the staff of the American Council on Education. We are especially indebted to Council President Logan Wilson, Vice-President Kenneth D. Roose, and David C. Nichols, assistant to the president, who served the Committee as staff director. Richard E. Peterson, of Educational Testing Service, helped to organize the work of the Committee. Alexander W. Astin, John Caffrey, W. Todd Furniss, and Richard A. Humphrey, all of the Council staff, made substantial contributions. Paul Tamminen helped to conduct liaison with student organizations. Elizabeth vanDuinen served efficiently as research assistant and Patricia A. Tatum capably tended to the secretarial details associated with the entire project. Special thanks are owed to Anthony E. Neville, of Baltimore, and Olive Mills, of the Council's staff, for editing the various manuscripts.*

A grant by the Mary Reynolds Babcock Foundation supported the work of the Committee; we are grateful to Dr. William C. Archie, executive director, for making it possible. —S. L.

BACKGROUND AND PURPOSE

"If colleges and universities will not govern themselves,
they will be governed by others."

THIS ELEMENTAL TRUTH was stated with urgency in April 1969, by the American Council on Education in *A Declaration on Campus Unrest*. Widespread disruption on the nation's campuses had angered the American public. As dissatisfaction grew, so did the specter of punitive measures: reduced financial support, restrictive legislation and harsh laws for handling even peaceful demonstrators, and political intervention in the affairs of educational institutions.

Convinced that the higher education community had to solve its own problems, the Board of Directors of the American Council on Education approved the establishment of a Special Committee on Campus Tensions in June 1969. The Committee, composed of lay leaders and spokesmen from the main segments of the higher education community and operating independently of the Council's regular organization, undertook to study campus tensions and to assist institutions in finding remedies.

The Committee sought out the widest feasible range of views about campus tensions and how conflicting points of view might be reconciled. To this end it did the following:

□ participated in a series of meetings with representatives of some fifteen associations in the field of higher education to elicit information and ideas for Committee consideration.

▢ commissioned more than twenty-five background papers by knowledgeable people in higher education, seeking especially their recommendations for reconciling campus conflicts.[1]

▢ sponsored a three-day workshop, organized and led by students, to discuss campus tensions as perceived by student leaders from colleges and universities around the country.

▢ commissioned special reports from three student organizations—the National Student Association, the National Association of Black Students, and the Association of Student Governments—and from individual students representing a wide range of opinion.

▢ undertook case studies of several institutions that have either experienced disruption and successfully coped with it or have, in other cases, instituted wide-ranging reforms without having experienced serious disruption.

▢ utilized the extensive research on campus unrest published by the American Council on Education and professional journals.

▢ consulted with presidents, trustees, and faculty at various institutions of higher education.

To all who have generously lent the benefit of their ideas and information, to all who have contributed their time to participate in Committee deliberations and the preparation of this report, the Special Committee on Campus Tensions is grateful. The Committee is, of course, solely responsible for the content of this report.

Members of the Committee come from many different sectors within and without the academic community and hold widely varying views on many subjects. In a report as long as this, about a subject as complex as this, not all members will agree with every statement made. Nonetheless, all are joined in general support of this report's conclusions and recommendations. Kingman Brewster, Jr., president of Yale University, originally served on the Committee but was unable to participate in drafting the report.

》　》　《　《

THIS REPORT is published at a time of great uncertainty about the future state of harmony or tension on the nation's campuses. The first half of the 1969-70 academic year was marked by apparent calm, and yet the arrival of spring signaled disruption that may, in total, surpass that of the record year, 1968-69.

Some observers have expressed the view to the Committee that the worst of the disruption lies behind us, or is a seasonal phenomenon. Others have warned that we are passing through the eye of the storm and that a more severe period of unrest lies ahead. While the Committee took no poll, most persons interviewed were uneasy about what the future might hold.

Violence and disruption (as defined in the study on which the following figures are based) have occurred on a minority of campuses. In the particularly turbulent year 1968-69, an estimated 145, or 6.2 percent, of the nation's 2,300 colleges and universities experienced incidents of violent protest; an additional estimated 379, or 16.2 percent, experienced nonviolent but disruptive protest.[2] Still, the majority of American college campuses have experienced at least one incident of protest, peaceful or otherwise.

While the statistics are cause for grave concern, we need to bear in mind that at most times and on most campuses disruption is not occurring. The news media, not surprisingly, focus upon incidents of disorder and ignore the campuses during times of tranquility.

Where disruption has occurred, it has generally been short-lived. When the demonstrators have gone home and the students have cleared out of the buildings, a few administrative positions may change encumbents, institutional policies may be altered, a few faculty members may leave, but on the whole universities retain their essential character. Classes are held, examinations are given, degrees are awarded, research grants are obtained, faculties meet and argue. Certainly the problem in the United States is far less severe than in some countries where universities are continually being disrupted.

Yet statistics about class hours interrupted or buildings occupied do not reveal the deeper crisis—confusion and uncertainty about the proper direction of change in higher education. There is abroad a feeling of the tide turning, a sense that a period is coming to an end and that a distinctively different one may be emerging. There is considerable doubt whether the future will be better than the past or, if better, how thoroughly we must discard old assumptions and verities to make it better. At the root of the crisis is the challenge to complacency and to the sanctity of tradition, and—now that the dissonant voices have been heard—the absence of accord among students, faculty, administrators, trustees, and the public generally, about where we go from here.

This report addresses itself to that crisis, though the purposes to be served are modest. The report is intended, first, to help bring about—both on and off college campuses—better understanding of the sources of discontent and conflict in American higher education. Second, the report is meant to provide college and university leaders with suggestions for fostering reconciliation, trust, and the conditions favorable to constructive change on the campus.

Chapter One
THE NATURE OF THE CRISIS

IN THE FALL of 1969, almost seven million students were attending about twenty-three hundred colleges and universities in the United States. More than two-thirds of those students were in publicly supported two-year, four-year, or graduate-level institutions. The rest were in private colleges and universities—some church-related, others independent. The campuses they attended ranged in enrollment from fewer than one hundred to more than forty thousand. The institutions varied in quality, in affluence, in faculty competence, in the academic aptitude of students. They varied in programs and purposes, as they varied also in the kinds of values, beliefs, and personal commitments characterizing their students and faculty.

There are two reasons for drawing attention to this diversity among the nation's colleges. First, the crisis in higher education is by no means uniform across the range of colleges and universities. Because only a minority of colleges have been scarred by disruptive incidents, the crisis may seem to have little pertinence, at least at present, for a majority of institutions and their students. There is widespread sympathy, nonetheless, among students for the aims of protestors, even though no more than 15 percent have been active in particular incidents.

Second, it should be understood that any analysis of campus unrest must necessarily be sketched in broad strokes —so broad that it cannot possibly be consistently cogent across the national spectrum of colleges and universities. Indeed, the combination of circumstances underlying a given confrontation on a given campus may be unique. The ideas to be put forth here for resolving potentially disruptive conflict, because of the differences in spirit and method of campus governance from one college to another, cannot be expected to apply to all institutions.

The first point is borne out by a closer look at the estimated 524 institutions that experienced at least one incident of violent or disruptive protest during 1968–69. From this, some generalizations can be drawn about the kinds of institutions in which disruption is most likely to occur.

Major protest incidents are about twice as likely to occur at private universities as at public universities. More than one in three of the private *universities* experienced violent protest during the 1968–69 academic year, while one in eight public universities experienced incidents of comparable severity. Approximately 70 percent of the private and 43 percent of the public universities experienced protest that was either violent or disruptive.

In general, the larger the institution, the more likely it will experience violent or disruptive protest. Very few institutions with enrollments under 1,000 had any incidents of violent protest in 1968–69. Among institutions of intermediate size (enrollments between 1,000 and 5,000 students), 4 percent of the two-year colleges, 5 percent of the four-year colleges, and 14 percent of the universities experienced violent protests. Of the large institutions (enrollment over 5,000), 16 percent of junior colleges, 14 percent of the senior colleges, and 22 percent of the universities experienced violent protests. There are also correlations with size when nonviolent disruptive incidents are considered.

The more selective a university, the more likely it will experience violent or disruptive protest. About 85 per cent of the most selective universities (those enrolling students of the highest academic ability) had disruptive incidents, of which 40 percent were violent and 45 percent nonviolent. Universities in the lowest category of selectivity experienced no such incidents. The association of selectivity with protest incidents was weaker among four-year colleges and was absent among two-year colleges.

》　》　《　《

A CLOSE LOOK at the colleges and universities that experienced violence or disruption during 1968–69 also reveals the kinds of issues that give rise to protest, how institutions typically respond to violence or disruption, and the consequences of violence or disruption upon the participants and the institutions.

Major protest incidents covered a wide range of student concerns. In 1968–69, student power was an issue in roughly three-quarters of the institutions experiencing violence or disruption. The most prevalent of the specific issues on campuses that had *violent* protest involved (1) instituting special educational programs for disadvantaged or minority groups, (2) allowing greater student participation on committees, (3) changing institutional disciplinary practices, (4) challenging apparent administrative indifference or inaction to grievances, and (5)—an off-campus issue—challenging alleged administrative indifference to local community problems. (We do not know, of course, the extent to which stated issues were truly the important issues or had wide student support.)

Among off-campus issues, leading to protest, those related to war have been prevalent. U.S. military policy—for example, in Vietnam, in regard to chemical-biological warfare, in deploying ABM's—was a reported issue in 38 percent of the institutions experiencing violence or disruption. Other military issues, such as ROTC programs and military research on campus, brought the total of war-related issues to roughly half the campuses that experienced violence or disruption.

Institutions have, in general, responded firmly to violence. Fifty-five percent of the institutions that experienced violence during 1968–69 had occasion to call in off-campus police. Roughly the same percentage of institutions report that some demonstrators were arrested. Some major civil or institutional action (arrest, indictment, dismissal, or suspension) was taken against individual students at three-fourths of the institutions where there were violent protests. (Similarly punitive measures were taken by 22 percent of the institutions that had nonviolent disruptive protests.) Sixty-two percent of the institutions report that administration or faculty negotiated issues with demonstrators when the protest was violent, but 83 percent negotiated when the protest was nonviolent.

Although unrest and change are positively associated, colleges and universities also have been instituting changes without confrontation and crisis. Most institutions reporting, including those where no major protest incidents occurred, made major changes in institutional policy and practices during 1968–69. Institutional changes were made as a direct result of protest activities at 72 percent of the campuses where protest was violent and at 54 percent of those where it was nonviolent but disruptive.

Campus tensions, with or without disruption, obviously have stimulated the processes of change. Changes not directly credited to protest incidents but possibly spurred by them were made at 80 percent of those institutions with violent protest, at 89 percent with nonviolent disruptive protests, and at 62 percent that experienced no major incidents. Changes were usually in the direction of increasing participation of students in institutional decision making, forming new committees or study groups, and making changes in curriculum.

» » « «

TO ACKNOWLEDGE, however reluctantly, that violence and disruption have sometimes been effective goads to institutional change is not to explain the current tide of violence and disruption on the nation's campuses. The colleges and universities, traditional bastions of rationality and civility, do not erupt in violence at the mere wave of a baton. Nor can student unrest be explained away as the modern-day equivalent of goldfish swallowing and the panty raid. Obviously something deeper and more disturbing is at work.

Serious and thoughtful explanations of current student unrest abound. To arrive at a better understanding about what the future may hold for colleges and universities, it will be helpful to review some of the major accounts of the underlying causes of student unrest. While there is considerable overlap among them, the theories can be conveniently divided into five general categories.

GENERATIONAL CONFLICT. In a historical study of student radicalism, *The Conflict of Generations,* Lewis S. Feuer makes Oedipal rebellion the basis for his explanation of student radicalism.[3] A generation gap exists, according to this hypothesis, in which youth rebel against the values and beliefs of their fathers and act out their disaffection by assaulting tradition and institutions, including universities.

Though popular, the generational conflict or Oedipal thesis has come under attack in recent research. Rather than being in revolt against parental beliefs, evidence shows, student activists are likely to share those beliefs and to enjoy close relationships with their parents. These findings, in turn, lead some to view student activism as an outgrowth of parental permissiveness in the upbringing of their children. But other studies show that student activists tend to come, not from permissive households, but from a highly principled family culture that emphasizes reasoning and persuasion as well as independence in thought and action. At present there is too little evidence to settle the issue.

SOCIAL "IRRELEVANCE" OF YOUTH. Many observers of the campus crisis have noted that, while American students are primarily rebelling against an unpopular war and social injustice for blacks, their counterparts in other countries are also in rebellion where there are no war or racial issues to stir up discontent. Searching for a common denominator of worldwide student revolt, some have speculated that youth in affluent societies are socially obsolescent, that they are kept too long in a state of dependence when what they most need is opportunity to feel socially and personally useful and "relevant." Bruno Bettelheim argues that adolescence is now prolonged beyond all reasonable limits. Too many "unwilling" youth, he says, are pushed into attending college by family aspiration and by social coercion to achieve white-collar status. This sense of irrelevance among youth is heightened, according to Bettelheim, by modern technology, which makes individual man and his work obsolete in the scheme of things. "Deep down, what youth is fighting against is not so much the war in Vietnam or the global balance, but an America whose technology seems to have robbed them of any place in the real work of the world." [4]

A related thesis is that attending college is, for many youth, an unsought experience. A distinguished university president, for instance, maintains that the crisis on the campus will not be relieved so long as students feel compelled to attend college for essentially nonintellectual reasons, such as satisfying parental longings, acquiring the credentials for "correct" careers, or avoiding the draft. Many believe that, somehow, attractive alternative options to attending college must be developed so that most of those who do become college students will do so for intellectual reasons.

OBSOLETE EDUCATIONAL PRACTICES. Any number of critics of higher education emphasize traditional educational practices as a contributing cause of campus unrest. The most radical of these critics argue that colleges and universities are structurally incapable of providing effective education in the modern age. These institutions, they say, have become socially dysfunctional—creating more problems than they solve. The admissions process, for example, which is inherently exclusive and tends to screen out blacks and other minorities, they cite as an elitist and therefore undemocratic tradition. Or, they sometimes argue, faculty members, by and large, are harmful to student learning because their world is detached from reality: what faculty know is largely irrelevant and how they teach it is generally obsolete. In a background paper prepared for the Committee, one adherent of this view argues that inasmuch as most colleges maintain walls between themselves and their environment, they are by definition socially irrelevant. Another calls the university a social parasite—a place where privileged people are maintained and perpetuate their own kind at the expense of the public purse. Still another, a faculty member, believes that soon professors, in the traditional mold, will become unnecessary to the educational process—except as counselors for students who will be teaching one another and learning experientially in the community. He concludes that, for most professors, the best they can hope for is to be phased out, mercifully.

More temperate critics of educational practices seek a middle ground between the status quo and a radical redefinition of the college, largely through increased provision for independent learning, more student initiative in curriculum design, experiential education, and a reduction of formal course requirements for degrees. One consultant to the Committee, noting that "the structure of special departments leaves too little room in the curriculum for the study of critical general problems such as racial injustice, urban chaos, and war, or perennial personal problems of sex, politics, and religion," urges the development of "relevant" liberal arts to prepare students as thoughtful citizens. He warns, however, that liberal education is no remedy for discontent but, instead, increases it. "For the liberal education of any person inherently creates something of a crisis of discontent, within himself if not within his family or community."

A BREAKDOWN OF LEGITIMATE AUTHORITY. There are some who believe that the crisis on the campus is best described as a crisis of legitimacy. Authority, as it has been traditionally held and exercised, no longer commands respect. A generation of students and young faculty has arisen that sees fit to take little for granted. Boards of trustees, because of their remoteness from the campus, are frequently viewed by students as not competent. Presidential and administrative authority and faculty hegemony in academic affairs are being attacked by dissatisfied students as self-serving and unresponsive to higher education's real needs. Thus, traditional mechanisms of campus governance are no longer appreciated, and many campus activists want, instead, direct participation or legitimate representation and truly responsive government.

There is widespread dissatisfaction with the outcome of learning and intellectuality. One consultant to the Committee expressed this with hyperbole: "It wasn't the Mississippi tenant farmer who ordered the troops to Vietnam. More likely, and more specifically, it was the Harvard Junior Fellows—those who had maximum chance to develop intellectually." He and others see a causal relationship between the higher learning, as currently purveyed, and dubious ends.

Much is also made of the experiential mode of learning rather than the traditional lectures and books. If the streets are better teachers than the classrooms, then why the classrooms? Why, indeed, a university? Both as to substance and process, the university has come to be viewed in some quarters as an expensive anachronism.

SOCIAL MALAISE THESIS. Perhaps the most popular thesis of all about the causes of tension on the campus is the one that closely links the university's troubles to the troubles of the society at large. Some students have perceived the university to be the handmaiden of a militarist and racist society. They see university complicity with the latter in selective admissions policies and inattention to "black studies" in the curriculum. They accuse the university of collusion with the military Establishment in ROTC programs, in classified war-related research, and in recruitment activities for the armed forces and corporations with military contracts.

In its extreme form, this view holds that America is a sick and unrescuable society, and all of its institutions—including colleges and universities—must be torn down. Other student activists see the campus as a base and starting point for nursing the society back to health. As the National Commission on the Causes and Prevention of Violence has noted, "They see the university, guardian of man's knowledge and source of his new ideas, as an engine for powering the reform of the larger society, and as the first institution they are in a position to reform." [5]

» » « «

WHATEVER one's view of the sources of campus unrest, unarguably the phenomenon cannot be ignored. Clark Kerr has compared campuses with the canaries that miners used to take down in the mines with them. Being somewhat more sensitive to bad air than the miner, the canary would keel over first, warning the miner he was in trouble. Whatever the toxins affecting the atmosphere of the nation's colleges and universities, they will ultimately affect the larger society as well.

It is important, therefore, to listen to the voices of students, faculty, administrators, and trustees on what has gone wrong in the colleges and universities.

Chapter Two

THE COLLEGIATE CONSTITUENTS: WHAT'S ON THEIR MINDS

MOST American college students view most of their collegiate experiences favorably. They find new interests in libraries, galleries, and laboratories, a range of intellectual and social models in the faculty and their fellow students, new ways to develop and test their academic and social skills, and greater freedom from conventional restraints than they have ever before experienced. In a world of options, the satisfied student believes that the choices he has made were, on the whole, better than alternatives he might have chosen. The results of research indicate that, on balance, most students find the college years rewarding.

Similarly, most faculty members seem to enjoy teaching or immersing themselves in research. Professors derive satisfaction from the successes of their best former students and are generally persuaded that their research results are important contributions to man's expanding body of knowledge. Though they have heard the assumptions of their worth challenged by student activists, most do not feel personally threatened, even when the din can be heard from the laboratory window.

Likewise, most college presidents and administrators seem to enjoy the challenges of their assignments. Even on the more placid campuses, of course, they face problems, even very pressing ones. But men and women do not enter positions of administrative responsibility blindly. Presidents of colleges and universities tend to be people of dedication and stamina who thrive on problems demanding solution. Even where the threat of violence or disruption is acknowledged, the Committee found, it is apparently not the problem foremost in the mind of the president.

Then there are the trustees. For them college and university problems tend to be a part-time, although very important, responsibility. Most trustees and regents believe in the worth of their involvement. They share with their presidents worries about the future of the institutions they serve. But, as the Committee also found, campus unrest is not foremost among their worries.

Nonetheless there is unrest, and it affects each of these four constituents. The academic community, the "community of scholars," today is a community divided. One of the most demoralizing aspects of the present divisions is an increase in the climate of fear on the campuses. Not only are campus communities often fearful of external pressures, but on many campuses radical groups have created an atmosphere where students are fearful of exercising independent judgment or defending points of view that are not fashionable. Furthermore, the students, the faculty, the administrators, the trustees, all have their deep discontents about the current functioning of colleges and universities. As often as not, these discontents have to do with the behavior and attitudes —or perceived behavior and attitudes—of one or more of the other constituents.

The purpose of this chapter is to present the concerns of some members of these groups about campus developments and tensions as they see them. (The Committee's reaction to these concerns will be voiced in the chapter on recommendations for resolving some of the problems.) Contradictory interests and points of view are evident in what follows. The objective of the next four sections, however, is not to pass judgment on allegations but to air the grievances of each party. It is the actions and reactions that follow from these discontents, after all, that constitute campus unrest.

A. WHAT'S TROUBLING THE STUDENTS

THOUGH A MAJORITY of American students are satisfied with most of their collegiate experience, there is in this observation no ground for complacency. Whatever the size of the discontented minority, its members are, as empirical studies have shown, among the brightest, most experienced, widely read, and articulate young Americans.

They are discontented, not only with colleges and universities, but also with American society, and they see a connection of basic failings between the two. For the most part, the dissatisfied young come from affluent homes; they are the "children of the American Dream," as one of their spokesmen says, and they are disenchanted with the Dream. They are joined in their expressions of discontent by the small but growing minority of college students who are black and are decidedly not the beneficiaries of the American Dream.

As the National Commission on the Causes and Prevention of Violence noted:

> Today's intelligent, idealistic students see a nation which has achieved the physical ability to provide food, shelter and education for all, but has not yet devised social institutions that do so. They see a society, built on the principle that all men are created equal, that has not yet assured equal opportunity in life. They see a world of nation-states with the technical brilliance to harness the ultimate energy but without the common sense to agree on methods of preventing mutual destruction.[6]

At the same time that students are eager to attack these problems, the Commission also noted, they face the prospect of being compelled to fight a war that many of them believe is unjustified.

In their view, the failings of American society are its propensity to violence, its exploitation of the weak, its indifference to human values, its hypocrisy, its corruption. Colleges and universities, say the discontented students, contribute to the corruption of the society by perpetuating and instilling in so-called leaders the values by which those leaders initiate (and gain from) external wars and internal repression, by which those leaders benefit from the status quo. Complicity with the corrupt order is seen in the sponsorship of military research and ROTC programs, in admissions policies that appear to be elitist and racist, in the choice of Establishment figures as trustees and college presidents.

» » « «

THIS INTERCONNECTION of discontents about the college and society may not be as neat as it appears. It is conceivable, for example, that many students dissatisfied with the society find the college a pleasant refuge from family antagonisms, community racism, police intimidation, or the intellectual sterility of their accustomed environments. Also, there are discontents about the college experience that do not translate, automatically, into discontents about the society.

It is axiomatic that the colleges and universities cannot cure all the ills that affect American society. They must, however, come to grips with the discontents of students, including those that have to do with institutional participation (or lack of it) in the pressing social issues. It is therefore necessary to explore the discontents that arise from direct student experience in the college and university.

INDIFFERENCE AND NEGLECT. A number of students have reported to the Committee their personal experience of indifference or neglect on the part of college and university faculties, administrators, and employees. Requests for information, they say, go unanswered; students wait endlessly to see officials; procedures are maintained for the convenience of the bureaucracy; appointments are not kept; class meetings are canceled at the whim of the instructor. Students can assume the existence of justifiable reasons for a few instances of this sort, but repeated failures to be noticed lead to resentment.

STEREOTYPES AND LABELS. Particularly on the larger campuses, students report that they are often treated as stereotypes rather than as individuals. Students complain that they are treated as immature, unskilled, incapable of exercising sound judgment even on matters most directly affecting their personal welfare. Inroads are being made against the old parietal rules governing social behavior, but on many campuses not fast enough to suit the students. Hair style and dress, for example, produce responses unrelated to the reasons students give for adopting a particular style: comfort, economy, association with a social group, or simply experiment. Student behavior that challenges old norms is castigated in state legislatures and newspaper editorials as "immature," "irresponsible," or often more opprobriously.

POLITICAL IMPOTENCE. A consequence of faculty and administrative attitudes that students are immature and irresponsible, say the students, is that they are denied their fair share in institutional governance. Proposals for representation on committees too often meet a reflexive "no" from administrators and faculty groups who have held the effective power. A common criticism of conventional student governments is that they concern themselves with trivia and that when they do attempt to deal with vital institutional issues, they encounter resistance.

LACK OF INFORMATION. Decisions depend upon information; good ones on accurate information. Students decide about academic programs and personal matters on the basis of college catalogs, other official printed sources, and information supplied orally by officials. Some students report to the Committee that they have been given inaccurate or incomplete information that adversely affects their college careers. Some contend that they were deliberately, rather than inadvertently, misinformed. In some cases, students told the Committee, information has been denied on the grounds that it is confidential or none of their business.

AVAILABILITY OF STUDENT RECORDS. At the same time that some students have challenged the right of institutions to keep information confidential, others have complained that their institutions have too widely distributed information about them. The supplying of grades and class standings to draft boards has been a bone of contention. Some students, especially radical leaders, say their actions and affiliations have been investigated by civil authorities with complete, enthusiastic cooperation from university officials.

DISCIPLINARY ACTION. Although the right of colleges to impose disciplinary penalties for academic transgressions and failures is not often challenged, in some circumstances particular punishments have become a source of discontent. Expulsion, which exposes the student to the draft, seems to many students a double penalty. In recent years, disruptive or destructive actions have seemed to students to bring excessive penalties; amnesty has often been one of their first demands in negotiating a truce.

POLICE ACTION. Apart from civil or academic penalties that may be imposed, many students report that the actions of local police or institutional security forces have been provocative. Two types of action are deeply resented. The more obvious is what they see as excessive force in restoring order. The other is harassment, which ranges from demanding identity cards from black but not white students, through continuing investigations, including wire tapping and surveillance, of some activist student leaders. Tense situations are sometimes aggravated by demeaning or illegal treatment of those arrested or detained.

DISCRIMINATION. Although most colleges and universities, by policy and regulation, prohibit discrimination based upon race, sex, economic standing, and religion, some students assert that they are victims of both institutional and individual discrimination. Evidences cited of institutional discrimination are de facto policies of social organization (for example, fraternities) permitted on campus, insufficient representation of minority groups on the faculty and the governing board, demonstrably lower average salaries for women employees, and the orientation of courses and texts to neglect minorities. On an individual basis, cases are cited of professors, administrators, students, and employees who express racial or other forms of prejudice openly. Women students complain that some professors treat them as if they were not suited for scholarly or professional roles.

BAD TEACHING. Complaints about teaching focus on both what is taught and how it is taught. The material taught, say students, is frequently out of date or simply wrong. Some instructors present the material, grade papers, and treat students in ways that are seen to be incompetent, offensive, or unfair. At particular issue is the absence of courses relating to the major social issues of our time.

INTIMIDATION. Some students see in the rewards and penalties attached to virtually all college regulations a basic system of threats. Violations of rules of conduct and failure to meet competitive standards may have severe consequences, the worst of which is expulsion. Thus, they feel, the basis of the institution's legitimacy is fear; and they resent having to work within the atmosphere they perceive.

FAIR PLAY AND DUE PROCESS. On campuses where the absolute authority of faculty and administration over student academic and social life has been a long-standing tradition, students maintain that the procedures for instituting change and for settling student grievances do not even respect the rights guaranteed in civil courts. Although customs and procedures are now being rapidly revised, the Committee has had reports of discontent arising out of flagrant denials of due process or refusal to consider the legitimate views of students on changes affecting their welfare.

INVOLUNTARY ATTENDANCE. A generalized discontent often accompanies students who are in college chiefly because of family pressures, or because they need to acquire a particular credential in order to enter the occupational field of their choice. Avoidance of the military draft all too often is a factor in a student's decision to attend or to remain in college.

Even among those who are voluntarily in college, a number report that they attend chiefly because it is the only place in our society that provides a social milieu in which they can be at all comfortable. Employers don't want them, they have no real responsibilities to family or local community, and only in colleges can they find a community of their peers. Academic programs and college-sponsored noncurricular activities hold no attraction: in order to join the community, however, they will play at book learning. For them, the future seems to offer little hope of improvement.

THE DRY RUN. It has been a tenet of many colleges that the institution offers the student an opportunity to experiment in many fields and make mistakes without suffering the consequences he would face outside college. A corollary is that the rewards of such a program are as insubstantial as the penalties. A number of students are discontented because the academic program denies them real rewards. They want to use their talents and energies on something that really counts: a beneficial change in the curriculum, improved living conditions, actual assistance to people in the local community, and the like.

INSTITUTIONAL RIGIDITY. Students frequently complain that whenever they air any of the above-mentioned grievances or propose reforms, the institutional machinery is unresponsive. Administrators, they say, are rigid in their policies, guarded and deceitful in their discussions with students, and "gutless" when confronted with major issues. Problems that are referred to faculty committees sink from view and are never resolved. When faculty committees do issue pronouncements, students contend, they usually defend the status quo. And in those instances when changes are recommended, it takes an inordinate amount of time to institute them. One student told the Committee that on his campus it takes two years to get a course removed from the curriculum, even when the main parties are agreed to such action.

» » « «

STUDENT PROPOSALS for changing colleges and universities cover a wide range. For some, the chief issue is the replacement of parietal rules by freedom to live and love where and with whom they wish. Others demand the reduction of formal academic requirements and the establishment of independent study. But there are also those, often highlighted by the communications media, who advocate the destruction of the university.

In governance, most proposals envision a reduction in the authority of administrators and trustees, and a corresponding increase in student power (and sometimes faculty power) through joint committees that would have control over most of the institution's functions. Some of these proposals include financial independence as a prerequisite to effective control, whether of a student organization or of an academic department.

Many suggestions deal with the establishment of detailed policies and procedures designed to ensure the student a fair ("constitutional") hearing in any disciplinary procedure.

Some, stressing the importance of reliable information in order to reach sound decisions, insist that all information about the institution be readily available to any student who requests it. On campuses where student participation in governance is not the issue, the lack of openness of faculty and trustee meetings frequently is an important issue.

Suggested modifications of academic programs ordinarily include less reliance on grades and testing, more freedom to choose courses that seem relevant to the students' interests, more freedom to create experimental courses, credit for work in a local community, and provision for closer association with faculty members than has been customary.

Suggestions for breaking ties with the evil in society are both negative and positive. Negatively, they urge that cooperation between the university and the military in war-related research and training be abolished; investments in enterprises identified with social repression be disposed of; practices which limit the advancement of ethnic minorities and women in universities and colleges be eliminated. On the positive side, students say that universities should actively seek to bring about desirable social change, not only in the field of civil rights and world peace, but also, more recently, in restoration and preservation of a decent physical environment. Students want the faculty and administrators to speak out as individuals on important public issues.

And finally, there are groups—small but articulate—who would require the university to lead a complete social revolution to destroy capitalism and existing institutions and replace them with a full egalitarian and more humane society. The university is chosen for this movement because it has by definition that part of the population most receptive to learning new ideologies. Such groups are now being challenged by more conservative students, not always of the far right. There is some statistical evidence that students are becoming more polarized in their opinions.

Almost everywhere, but especially on the larger campuses, students are asking that university officials, and particularly the faculty, show personal concern about them as individuals, rather than treating them as clients, customers, or nuisances.

B. WHAT'S TROUBLING THE FACULTY

THE CONCERNS troubling the faculty community are, similarly, many and various; they differ according to the kind of faculty, the kind of institution, and the ascendant issues of the moment. It is not surprising that the more conservative responses to university problems tend to come from the senior faculty, who obviously have a greater vested interest in current practice and are especially critical of the trend toward more permissive curricula. Besides the senior faculty, there are the department chairmen with their special role, and then the junior faculty and teaching assistants. It is from the latter two groups that the most outspoken criticism of the university has come. Significantly the data from one American Council on Education study indicate that faculty were involved in the planning of more than half of the recent protests.[7]

The more prestigious and elite universities, generally having the largest representation of outspoken faculty and students, experience the most campus unrest. Although most of the unrest has been associated with the multifunction universities, the four-year state colleges and four-year private liberal arts colleges, too, are coming in for their share of dissatisfactions. Faculty tensions are evident in the four-year state colleges for a variety of reasons, among them pressure to become universities with prestigious graduate programs and the desire of faculty to broaden their participation in governance. Faculty in the four-year private liberal arts colleges also face a series of pressures: anxiety over their lack of status as compared to faculty in a university and, for many, a fear for the survival of their college. Faculty in community and junior colleges face the enormous pressures of growth and changing status, but these institutions traditionally have had much less faculty-student involvement in the decision-making process.

» » « «

RECOGNIZING, THEN, that distinctions must be drawn among the kinds of faculty and the kinds of institutions, it is still possible to identify major problems and issues creating faculty tensions and dissatisfactions. These include the governance and administration of institutions, the functioning of departments, certain basic academic questions, relationships with students, and finally, the goals and objectives of the university.

GOVERNANCE AND ADMINISTRATION OF THE INSTITUTION. Faculty are exerting pressure for more involvement in determining the broader purposes of the institution and more control over the conditions affecting their work. Paralleling student demands, faculty activists want a more important role or association with governing bodies, including the trustees. There is an accelerating move toward organization for collective bargaining, especially in two-year institutions, but to an extent in four-year institutions as well. The general dissatisfaction of faculty with the effectiveness of the administrative process grows during periods of tension. For instance, it has been observed that as an aftermath of major confrontations, faculty frequently blame the administrators for the conduct of the negotiations and the handling of the disputes; a consequence is sometimes the departure of the administrative officers involved.

THE FUNCTIONING OF DEPARTMENTS. Under fire, especially from younger faculty, are procedures and standards for determining tenure, promotion, salaries, teaching assignments, and departmental growth. Younger faculty are demanding a greater part in these decisions than the present concept of seniority allows. Some are disturbed by what they consider to be the excessive emphasis upon research and publications, at the expense of teaching. The university, they charge, is hypocritical when it insists that teaching is the first priority but then rewards the researcher, the administrator, and the publishing scholar with markedly higher salaries than the dedicated and skillful teaching faculty member. Some believe that all professors at the same grade and with the same number of years of service should receive the same salary. One consultant to the Committee argued that professors of law and medicine should receive the same pay as professors of English; persons teaching the history of nineteenth-century France should be rewarded as well as those teaching biochemistry.

Some senior scholars, on the other hand, are forecasting the withdrawal of major research efforts from large universities and the establishment of outside research institutions or agencies so that scholars can be sheltered from the counterproductive interruptions of students and younger faculty.

ACADEMIC QUESTIONS. Younger faculty members have joined students in demanding more interdisciplinary work, new ethnic study programs, and broader representation on the faculty, particularly of blacks and women. Present standards for faculty and academic programs, they assert, are antiquated and cannot meet the needs of present-day students. With respect to interdisciplinary work, many younger faculty strongly resent departmental rigidity and the resistance to providing adequate support for the broader areas of educational concern. Faculty members disagree on the structure of ethnic study programs: some give strong support to student demands for control of content and appointment of personnel; others resist just as strongly in the interest of academic standards and academic freedom.

Questions of external threats to academic freedom also loom very important in the anxieties of the faculty, both senior and junior. This anxiety is prevalent among faculty members in institutions that are under vigorous attack from the legislature, the public, and even their own boards of control. These faculty members are alarmed at the intervention of public authorities and politics into university administration and feel the need for more effective rebuttal of unsupported charges.

RELATIONS WITH STUDENTS. Students who demand more contact with their instructors and more of a role in determining the character of their own academic programs have begun to wear out their welcome. Faculty members complain that today's students are exceedingly demanding of their time, and that student-faculty committee deliberations tend to go on endlessly. Faculty serving jointly with students on committees, having devoted countless hours to debate and to the preparation of reports, finally assert that they are weary— they have had it and want to get back to their own research and educational interests. Yet the agreements reached with a given group of students often may not be satisfactory to the next student class, so that the process of give-and-take with students must be carried out over and over again. Some faculty are beginning to refuse to pay the personal price being exacted by the system of participatory democracy.

Other faculty members are seeking ways of avoiding student debate, less because of the protracted character of the discussion than because of the lack of civility and the intemperateness of the encounter. As one faculty member puts it: "The withdrawal thus far is largely due to changes in the style of debate, and to a distaste for threats and personal abuse in the gutter language sometimes employed by radical students to whom civility and rational discourse are contemptible middle-class evasions." [8]

Still other faculty are resentful of student attempts to determine the content of curricula and academic programs, on the ground that students are a transitory element in the university. Some would concede an advisory role to students, but scarcely more than that. Faculty, they say, have the competency to make curricular judgments; they also provide continuity in the university.

GOALS AND OBJECTIVES OF THE UNIVERSITY. Great and growing discontent is being expressed by segments of the faculty over the priorities of the university as they affect current commitments, new fields, and new approaches to education. Faced with genuine uncertainty about the goals and objectives of the university, often lacking educational leadership from administrative quarters, the faculty find themselves caught in the cross-fire between the conservative public and student activists.

The prevailing inability of the faculty to speak with a united voice betrays the sharp divisions within their ranks. The young faculty accuse their elders of opting for the status quo to preserve their power and position. Yet it is probably closer to the truth to say that the paralysis of the faculty in some institutions reflects organizational inflexibility; in others it stems from genuine ideological disagreements within the faculty membership. Although college faculties are more liberal politically than the general public, the generalization disguises the spectrum of opinion likely to be represented on a faculty. Once these differences were aired in polite conversation at the faculty club; nowadays, as students and faculty activists stage confrontations and demand institutional commitments on social issues, individual faculty members tend to identify themselves with one camp or another. Moreover, younger faculty members are rankled by the seeming fogyism of their elders, at the same time that senior faculty are genuinely shocked by the disrespect for "objective scholarship," the indifference to scholarly detachment, and the incivility being manifested within their own ranks.

» » « «

THE CLEAVAGE between the faculty members of the left and the right helps explain the intensity of faculty disputes over many of the issues discussed here but it does not account completely for all the conflicts. For example, conservative faculty, more often than not, can be found supporting student charges that the teaching function has been downgraded in favor of research and publication. Care must be taken, therefore, not to place exclusive emphasis on differences in political and social opinion on the campuses as the explanation for faculty discontent.

C. WHAT'S TROUBLING THE ADMINISTRATORS

IN 1949 the president of the University of Wyoming defined the essential qualifications for his job:

> A college or university president is expected to be an educator, a scholar, an administrator, a business man, a public speaker, a writer, a politician, a giver of dinners, a charmer at receptions, a moral force in the community, a commentator on national and international affairs, and popular with students, faculty and alumni.[9]

If that was a prescription for a superhuman being twenty years ago, consider the expectations that are piled upon the college president today. Faculty members expect him to raise their salaries, provide more facilities for research, and give them a stronger voice in making policy. The students hold the president responsible for instituting reforms and increasing student freedom. Trustees and state legislators press him to economize. The alumni expect him to field winning athletic teams and to preserve the values they remember from their days as students.

The president is generally held responsible for dissatisfactions and for whatever can go wrong, and when mistakes are made, he may be the first casualty. If he fails to keep costs down, to control unruly student rebels, or to keep the faculty happy, he becomes the scapegoat and may be summarily sacrificed.

Increasingly, presidents point out that their capacity to do anything that "makes a difference" is seriously impaired by the complexity and tortoiselike pace of consensual processes. On the other hand, if a president acts too swiftly or does not consult enough people, he will find himself cut off from his potential support.

Also, administrators in increasing numbers are called upon to negotiate issues, and to negotiate in a style that is new to the college campus. Impossible demands are labeled "nonnegotiable" at the outset. Parties to the dispute do not play by the old rules or by any rules at all, and this anomaly of governance is especially disconcerting to a man trained to reason and to accord respect to his adversary. Moreover, men who over the years have learned how to solve most familiar problems now find themselves forced to share their authority, their political views (and sometimes their offices) with students and other juniors who might have been expelled or dismissed in an earlier decade.

For all these hardships, in times of turmoil, the president is likely to be alone. One executive, who became the target of disrupters, observed angrily, "No one was in sight when it came time for support. Everyone faded away into the background. It was like a gigantic live replay of the movie 'High Noon.' All the so-called friends had reason to be absent on the day of the showdown."

» » « «

THIS IS THE POSITION in which a great many presidents and administrators find themselves. What are the particular issues that bother them? The Committee asked some sixty top officers of American colleges and universities to state the "worst one or two persistent problems which create or increase tension on your campus."

The sixty administrators represent a sample of large and small, public and private, old and new colleges and universities. From these responses the most obvious conclusion is that there is no simple consensus. Sources of irritation and tension on the campus reflect the whole domain of the president's ultimate responsibilities.

FACULTY. Leading the tallies is the faculty: many respondents mention this constituent as one or another source of difficulties. Even here, however, there is no ready consensus (perhaps a reflection of the differences among institutions). One president complains of the "unwillingness or inability of the faculty to adjust to change," another of "suffocating academic arrogance." While a number of presidents see the faculty as the entrenched voice of conservatism on the campus, others are disturbed by the active role of faculty in promoting dissent and divisiveness. One is vexed by "faculty members who encourage students, by positive efforts or lack of enough guts to oppose, in their efforts to politicize the university." Another notes that tenured faculty are participating in "whispered harassment of the president and his office (or other administrative offices) by SDS-type student groups."

FINANCIAL DIFFICULTIES. Since institutional change almost invariably translates into new expenditures of funds, it is not surprising that money is a frequently cited worry among college presidents. "The financial crunch," adds one president, is "pervasive and real, but few are ready to believe that. So innovations except those which cost enormous amounts of new money are not yet the fashion."

COMMUNICATION. Mentioned as frequently as financial difficulties are problems of communication. Within the academic community, failures of communication are manifested both in misunderstandings and in lack of understanding of why things are as they are. One president complains about "having to decide so many things repeatedly—always taken up de novo—as though the issue had no history and had not been considered or decided before."

Among the agents of misinformation noted by administrators are the campus newspaper and the public media—

newspapers and television. The effect of misinformation, one respondent notes, is that "we are constantly having to re-assure people that we are not planning to do things we have never dreamed of doing, in the face of supposedly informed rumors to the contrary."

Commenting at length on communication problems, another expressed the view that not all failures are inadvertent:

> Administrative and trustee statements are very frequently misinterpreted, as the result of really . . . paranoid efforts on the part of students and faculty to discover a plot where there is none. Students distrust trustees and administrators and faculty; faculty distrust students, administrators and trustees; trustees distrust faculty and students, and so on. All this happens despite the fact that there is an abundance of information, which all too many people either choose to ignore entirely or twist to fit their preconceived notions.

GOVERNANCE. A good many replies could be tallied under this loose heading, but to lump them together as defining a single problem would be misleading. The targets of criticism, for example, varied. Faculty were criticized for their "persistent unwillingness . . . to involve students in some of their hallowed preserves." Students were criticized for their "unilateral demands" and their "constant pressure to erode one rule and regulation and policy after another." One respondent was especially critical of the board of trustees: "Either they cause problems by an excessive concern about events on the campus or they limit our options in advance, or they second-guess our decisions in such a way as to limit our options in the future. Most of the problems we have had would have been less aggravated and others would not have arisen had it not been for the board."

Another criticized those of his fellow administrators who cling to an "authoritative style of management." Administrators were also criticized for their willingness to see "faults and shortcomings of colleagues but not their own."

Most college presidents would probably agree with the observation that there is a "confusion of roles in the performance of responsibilities." While some complained of important decisions being made without presidential consultation, another noted that "consultation is grinding us to a halt." The worst problem, according to one respondent, "is the increasing authority of faculty and students with no increase in responsibility, and at the same time, the lessening of the authority of the president with no change in his responsibility."

There was a time, a president noted, when a consensus about goals allowed institutions to operate under a set of informal understandings, with little need to spell out formal authority. "Now we are in a day when this consensus no longer exists and in which institutions are thus going to have to spell out their governmental arrangements in some detail and to provide for the contingency that they may have to exercise formal authority and even to impose sanctions."

INSTITUTIONAL GOALS. Although the connection with immediate tensions was not always made clear, there were many expressions of concern about disagreements or vagueness in defining institutional goals and standards. "The major and very pervasive problem," one respondent summed up, "is the lack of agreement as to the nature of the university and its role in the area of social and political change." While one president saw the essential division of agreement on goals as lying between faculty and students, another pointed to the "erosion in the cohesiveness of the faculty in its attitude toward institutional goals and appropriate means of achieving them.

STUDENT UNREST. A surprisingly small number of respondents mentioned what is so often thought of in connection with campus tensions, namely, violence and disorder. Most concerns were practical: how to deal with threats of disruptive protests, how to improve relations between students and local civil authorities, how to cope with "student arrogance, upstartism, and bad manners."

Some expressed specific concern about the tensions generated by the presence of minority-group students and the need to develop effective educational opportunities for these students. Among those who spoke of these problems, most recognize the need to take steps to increase educational opportunities for minority groups. Still, said one, there is the possibility of "unforeseen incidents triggering a protest by black students." One respondent described the basic problem this way: "The need for both blacks and whites is to forget that the black man is 'black'."

The remainder of the problems and tension-generators scattered over a wide field. Among those mentioned by respondents were the Vietnam war, intercollegiate athletics, predictions of student enrollments, the threat of a student rent strike, "two or three busybody alumni."

» » « «

THE PREVAILING IMPRESSION these responses leave is one of recognition of the enormous tasks of great scope and complexity facing administrators at the same time that resources are inadequate and the academic community seems unwilling to pull together toward common goals. Countering this tone, however, is the tone of resolution of men who believe affirmatively in the contributions their institutions can make to the larger society.

Though presidents may seem to scatter the fire of their complaints and criticisms in all directions in return for the pressures which seem to come to them from all directions, few of them abandon hope in the ultimate victory of reason, of compromise and consensus. Many feel that the

troubles of recent years will ultimately produce change in
desirable directions.

D. WHAT'S TROUBLING THE TRUSTEES

TRUSTEES, who presumably represent the public interest and
embody "lay control" of the institution, soon discover (if
they did not already know it) that, especially in time of crisis,
an academic community is not a readily coordinated enterprise. Many competing interests clamor for recognition and a
share of scarce resources; the trustees have the ultimate responsibility for determining (broadly or in detail, depending
on the institution) which interests coincide with the institution's best interest and can be served with the funds available.

Conserving and increasing the material assets of an educational institution, overseeing the improvement of its programs, maintaining its coherence and integrity, and protecting it against destructive forces are tasks that try the mettle
of trustees almost everywhere. Today, as never before, they
are called upon to represent the public's interest to institutions, and the interests of institutions to the public.

» » « «

TO FIND OUT the concerns now uppermost in the minds of
trustees, a query was addressed to board chairmen of a
variety of institutions across the country. More than fifty
replied, and some did so at length. (Though a representative
sampling was sought, the replies do not, of course, speak for
all trustees.)

If the replies are a reliable guide, trustees are aware that
in some quarters the legitimacy of their authority is being
attacked, their qualifications and organizational composition
questioned, their performance criticized, and the importance
of their function denigrated. In a paper prepared for the
Committee, one trustee began by showing sensitivity to the
range of attitudes about trustees, as illustrated by his selection of quotations.

> A board of regents, representative of the university con-
> stituency, is more important now than at any time in
> the history of higher education. (*A business executive*)

> Boards of trustees and regents are an anachronism, and
> should be abolished, if not immediately, certainly over
> the next five years! (*A graduate student from a West
> Coast university*)

> It's about time regents helped constituencies under-
> stand the revolutionary changes taking place in aca-
> demic life and not simply interpret what they think are
> our wishes to the academic community. (*An attorney*)

Trustees are old, rich, totally out of touch with today's academic world and useless except for fund raising. (*An undergraduate student leader in a private Midwestern college*)

Students and faculties are now so irresponsible and militant that trustees have an obligation to demonstrate who holds the actual power. *We* hold it, not the faculty, not the president, not the students, and it is time we started making that clear! (*Trustee of an Eastern college*)

Although there is manifest disagreement about whether trustees are really needed and, if needed, about their duties and how they should be executed, it is nonetheless evident that leaders among them are deeply concerned with a wide range of critical problems in American higher education. According to the recent inquiry, the six most common concerns of trustees (in descending order of frequency) are: (1) finances, including optimum use of funds and facilities, and threatened loss of support as a result of public backlash; (2) governance, including communication; (3) faculty, teaching, and innovative educational programs; (4) student unrest; (5) definition of institutional goals and higher education's relations to society; (6) institutional leadership.

FINANCES. Since the public interest in higher education bears very directly on financial support, trustees, as representatives of that interest, are necessarily concerned with money matters.

The most prevalent single worry of trustees and regents today is the growing public disenchantment with higher education, and the prospective leveling-off or even decline in financial support as a result of reaction to campus disorders. Many of the proposed reforms that come before them call for added expenditures in a period of financial stringency; seldom do student or faculty recommendations for change suggest what their proponents would be willing to forgo in order to acquire the often expensive new "goodies." Moreover, urgings that academic institutions develop action programs to help solve problems of environmental pollution, poverty, slums, the culturally deprived, and so on, come at a time when these very problems compete with educational needs for financial support.

Trustees of independent colleges and universities are bothered about the future of private higher education. Board members in both the private and public sectors report being plagued by the consequences of inflation, loss of federal grants, student aid difficulties, soaring construction costs, and continued pressures to broaden services without regard to the limited means available. Trustees also worry (more than other members of the academic community tend to do) about wasteful duplication of facilities and programs.

GOVERNANCE. While, in general, trustees oppose the inclusion of faculty and students in their membership because of possible conflicts of interest and the inherent cleavages in special pleading, many acknowledged need for better bases of board selection and diversity among members.

Insofar as relations between the board and the faculty are concerned, a trustee of a major university asserted that the rhetoric of faculty governance betrays a cultural lag. Intricate structures maintain a pretense of a self-governing "community of scholars," where there is no real community. Except in crisis, he continued, most professors do not want to be bothered by problems of academic government. They rise in protest and then lapse back into their own affairs, leaving day-to-day government to a small minority—mostly the bureaucrats and politicians in their midst. By implication, in large and complex institutions where the concept of "community" has lapsed, responsibility has to be assumed somewhere—not just for parking, money raising, and public relations, but for the "deeper requirement of any organization for central direction." Most trustees argue that they and their chief executive officer, the president, often have no option but to carry out this responsibility.

THE FACULTY AND TEACHING. Trustees are concerned not only about faculty derelictions in self-governance but also by the high proportion of campus disruptions in which members of the teaching staff (mostly the younger and lower-ranked members) take part. Trustees are also prone to interpret the first loyalty of many academicians to their discipline or field as a sign of disloyalty to the institution.

As one survey shows, more than nine out of ten trustees believe that the teaching function is more important than research. Many of them worry about the priority given to research and publication as a basis for professional recognition, and want to strengthen the significance of effective teaching in the institution's reward scheme. Likewise, they have increasing doubts about tenure, viewing it as a shield for neglect and incompetence, rather than simply a protection of academic freedom. Some share with student dissidents a feeling that many faculty are opposed to innovation and change in their own areas, are not really zealous about the improvement of teaching and learning, and are reluctant to have their real productivity evaluated.

Since they believe that everything else in an institution is subsidiary to the educational program, trustees view the ultimate responsibility of a board as necessarily implying a deep concern for basic academic functions.

Thus they complain about having programs reported to them only in financial terms and about receiving information on educational developments that have already taken place. Even board members who wish to effect what they regard as constructive changes are uncertain how to proceed in the face of faculty indifference or opposition to lay interference.

STUDENT UNREST. It will perhaps surprise some to learn that concern with student unrest ranked only fourth as a current worry among the trustees queried.

In one highly selective private institution, an uppermost concern pertained to pressures pushing that institution more and more toward serving "the alienated affluent and the alienated impoverished." Several trustees expressed puzzlement over dual admissions standards to enroll disadvantaged students, and also doubted whether most institutions would or could provide the added funds, facilities, staff, and special programs to meet their needs. One commentator, speaking broadly, observed that the large majority of institutions are designed to serve only one of three types of students—the 70 percent who adjust to the curriculum and instruction without being very creative or imaginative. The ill-served groups (approximating the remaining 30 percent) are the underendowed or disadvantaged and, at the other extreme, the highly intelligent and creative.

Other trustees voiced astonishment and dismay about students' motives and philosophies, and a concern, already indicated, about whether adverse public reaction will be reflected in greatly curtailed financial support of both public and private institutions.

INSTITUTIONAL GOALS AND SOCIETAL RELATIONS. Most trustees appear to be well aware of their obligation to help relate institutional objectives to the needs and aspirations of the supporting society. They reject the idea that the college or university is an organization intended solely to meet the needs of individual students as defined by the students themselves. They also resist the syndicalist view of some professors that the academic profession should control virtually all of the educational aspects of institutions of higher learning. Some trustees regard presidents and other officers of top administration as being primarily executives of broad policies formulated by trustees.

Despite this desired primacy, trustees are more often validators than formulators of policy. "In fact," one observer has noted, "it can be said that most institutions operate by habits, by assumptions, by accumulated decisions—all acquiring in the course of time the force of common law. But the vulnerability of institutions to attacks by radical minorities has been dramatized by the revelation that boards have not adequately devoted themselves to the review and refinement of policies and to the effective communication of policy."

Trustee comments repeatedly show a felt need to clarify the objectives of American higher education as a whole and the role of each institution within the system. Many realize that traditional programs do not always fit current needs, and that better institutional guidelines should stem from long-range planning and the establishment of campus priorities. They sense that the heightened importance of higher education and the prospect of its becoming universal will thrust most colleges and universities into a closer relationship with the surrounding society. They have a growing awareness that in many places compromises will have to be worked out between competing conceptions of the college or university as a community of scholars, a community of students, a corporate enterprise, an agency or arm of the state, a public service agency, and so on. Charged with maintaining the solvency and protecting the integrity of their institutions, they also worry about upholding these responsibilities while simultaneously responding to an increased variety of internal pressures and being party to the allocation of scarce resources to social problems of the larger society.

INSTITUTIONAL LEADERSHIP. By and large, trustees are of the opinion that individual leaders are no less essential than individual institutions to the welfare of American higher education. Trustees of public institutions, in particular, view with some alarm the tendency of politicians and bureaucrats in the national capitol and in state capitols to bypass and undermine the traditional powers of trusteeship and to erode the leadership responsibilities of the executive officers the boards have chosen. Trustees see the main responsibilities falling upon themselves and the presidents—to provide creative leadership and not just mediation, moderation, or conciliation.

Some board members concede that a reexamination of trustee functions is overdue. They acknowledge their shortcomings in dealing with many of the complexities of institutional governance, and believe, further, that better liaison is required with faculty, students, and administrators. They also acknowledge the need for improved methods of selecting board members, better devices for effecting change as well as continuity in their membership, more effective ways of perceiving the right questions and getting the right answers about the institutions they oversee. Even though they grant that their changing assignments may call for more diversity of talent and experience, they oppose the idea that a governing board should be a collection of special representatives.

As one prominent board member has put it, "Trustees should not run the institution, but should see that it is well run." Most trustees realize the need to delegate many of their powers to the president, and to hold him responsible for the execution of basic policies. In this same vein, nine out of ten trustees view the president as a leader rather than a mere mediator. Although they sometimes feel that presidents and other administrative officers are not sufficiently firm-handed in what they regard—in corporate terminology —as "management," many are aware that the central direction of academic enterprise must depend more upon persuasion than dictation in situations where shared power, consultation, and the development of consensus are the most effective means to institutional ends.

Chapter Three

RECOMMENDATIONS

THE HIGHER EDUCATION community cannot realistically hope to solve all the problems that create campus tensions. It cannot alone stop war, eliminate poverty, rebuild cities, or expunge racism. It cannot afford to be indifferent to these problems, however, if only because campus turmoil is not likely to cease unless genuine progress is made toward curing the glaring social ills. The war in Vietnam and the draft system, in concert, contribute heavily to campus unrest. Until the nation ceases to force young men to fight in a war they believe unjust, a major source of campus tensions will remain. For the campus to be a haven for those who wish to avoid military service is an inequity of the draft system and a perversion of educational purpose.

Through educating decision-makers, conducting research, diffusing knowledge, and proposing solutions to social problems, our colleges and universities can have a considerable, if not decisive, influence on the decisions that affect the nation's quality of life. In each of these roles, colleges and universities serve society best by giving prime allegiance to truth. Truth-seeking, in turn, requires conclusions openly arrived at and receptivity to new ideas. First and foremost, then, our colleges and universities must be centers of free inquiry.

Efforts to politicize colleges and universities risk public reprisals with consequent restrictions on free inquiry. Legislative moves in this direction, at both state and federal levels, are already deeply disturbing. Likewise, demands made on the campus through intimidation or violence are inimical to the spirit of free inquiry. The search for truth is the first casualty.

Political exploitation of campus problems by some public figures has become one of the sources of polarization on the campus. Public officials and others having the public's attention should gauge their response to campus disruption by recognizing that repressive and provocative pronouncements by those in authority may have the same inflammatory effect that extremist rhetoric has on the campus.

Campus violence already threatens some colleges and universities with repressive forces that could cripple their freedom for many years to come. Even so, this Committee is mindful of the dangers in laying out inflexible guidelines about unacceptable conduct or in specifying the precise moment when the hazard to the institution is such that civil authorities must be called upon. The questions have been studied in detail by the Commission on Campus Government and Student Dissent of the American Bar Association, which isssued its report in February.[10]

What, then, in view of their limited powers, can colleges and universities do about problems arising from campus tensions? At the outset, let it be noted that campus tensions are not necessarily harmful to higher education. It is the responses to tensions that lead to constructive or destructive outcomes. As one Committee consultant put it, "If there were no tensions on campus, there should be a committee established to create some, because a campus without tensions is intellectually moribund." Present campus tensions, therefore, provide an opportunity and an impetus for some overdue reforms in higher education. As the discontents of students, faculty, administrators, and trustees (expressed in chapter 2) make clear, almost everyone agrees that change is necessary in higher education.

It is equally clear that these four groups are not of one mind about the nature of campus problems, how to solve them, or who should solve them. Trustees are commonly assumed to stand firmly for order and against disruption, undisturbed by pressures until things seem to be getting out of hand. Reform proposals intended to alleviate student and faculty malaise seldom take account of trustees' worries about scarce resources, or even acknowledge that such worries exist. Faculty members, on the other hand, appear to be more directly involved in the internal issues besetting the campuses. Nevertheless, there is considerable difference of faculty opinion about steps to resolve controversies. In academic matters the interests of junior and senior scholars often conflict. Many of the former desire both participation in decision making and a redress of the balance between research and teaching. Though some faculty want to add colleagues having different political and social outlooks, others oppose strenuously what they regard as a political test for employment. Students on their part are also becoming increasingly divided, between those who are heavily involved in political issues on or off campus and those who resent interference with their professional and vocational preparation.

This Committee's recommendations cannot reconcile all the conflicting values and viewpoints. Nevertheless, we believe these recommendations respond to legitimate concerns; if given wide campus support, they can mitigate unrest by improving the conduct of the educational enterprise. Their adoption and, more important, their effectiveness once adopted, presuppose that the entire academic community must share and abide by certain principles—among them fair play, civility, concern for the individual, care in interpreting evidence, respect for privacy, equity in administering penalties, and faith in rational discourse.

The recommendations deal first of all with the roles and responsibilities of students, faculty, administrators, and trustees, then with general matters of governance and institutional goals.

STUDENTS

Colleges and universities exist primarily for the education of students. Society assigns to these institutions no task more important than providing students the opportunity to ripen their intellectual and creative capacities, learn from the heritage of the past, and develop themselves as responsible citizens.

Student critics object to the current emphasis on a "manpower" perspective. They object to being shaped for slots in a less than ideal social order. Our institutions indeed must prepare trained manpower for a complex society. All the same, greater weight should be given to educating young people to realize more fully their own potentials on their own terms, and to help them find new solutions to the urgent social problems of our times. Here education, not just training, is clearly at issue.

Educational institutions foster the development of responsible adults by assigning real responsibilities to students to the extent of their capabilities and willingness to assume responsibility. They may hamper and retard that development by following policies of in loco parentis in regard to parietal rules (now on the wane) or policies that "the faculty knows best" in regard to the curriculum and other matters central to the institution's purposes (much less effectively challenged). For colleges and universities to provide effective educational environments for the development of competence and maturity, new policies are required. In wise balance, these policies give young people a more responsible role in the educational decisions affecting them, while at the same time acknowledging greater adult competence and greater investment in institutional continuity on the part of the faculty and administration. The wise balance called for is, obviously, not easily identified or achieved.

Although forceful measures are sometimes unavoidable when campus disruption goes to intolerable extremes, the use of force is basically undesirable. Punitive measures tend to foster—when they work—dependent compliance rather than responsible commitment. Firmness of policy needs to be balanced by openness and flexibility. If students are to be held accountable for their actions, they should have a voice in determining the permissible limits of their actions.

1. Students not only should be given substantial autonomy in their nonacademic activities, but should also participate in matters of general educational policy, especially in curricular affairs. Since increased participation will contribute to effective institutional decision making and is also of educational benefit, students should serve in a variety of roles on committees that make decisions or recommendations. In some nonacademic areas students should have effective control; in some general educational policy matters they should have voting participation; in other matters, they should act in an advisory or consultative capacity. Effective student respresentation will not only improve the quality of decisions; it will also help to ensure their acceptability to the student body.

2. As institutions give up policies of in loco parentis in response to students' educationally valid wishes for independence, students must know that they cannot be effectively shielded from the consequences of their behavior, especially when it violates the laws of society at large. The abandonment of parietal rules, however, does not relieve institutions of the need to have effective self-government. The more effective the self-government, the less frequently and abrasively will police and other agencies of the society intrude on the campus.

3. Colleges and universities should regularly review, with legal counsel, their practices regarding such matters as the confidentiality of information about students and the privacy of student living quarters. They should also review their provisions for due process in disciplinary proceedings. These proceedings need not have, in every case, the formal, adversary aspects of a courtroom trial. But the option of formal proceedings should be open to any student whose future could be seriously affected by the outcome of a disciplinary decision.[10]

4. Students who want to propose changes in institutional practices or policies (as differentiated from asking redress of particular grievances) should be given the opportunity to learn in advance the institution's decision-making process that applies to their proposal. They should also consider thoroughly the evidence and arguments supporting their proposal and anticipate questions that will be raised by others, including fellow students. A well-considered pro-

posal often grows out of preliminary discussion with faculty and administrators.

5. Students must recognize and respect the rights and privileges of their fellow students as they seek rights and privileges for themselves. These include First Amendment rights of free speech and peaceable assembly, the right to pursue without hindrance one's course of study, and the privilege of experimenting with ways of thinking, both conventional and unconventional. Threats, violence, coercive disruption of classes or lectures, and similar acts that tread upon the rights of others are intolerable.

6. To a very great degree institutional functioning depends upon the voluntary self-discipline of the students. On the other hand, in several institutions, overt threats of violence and personal injury to students and others by individuals on and off campus have had destructive effects upon disciplinary proceedings as well as the process of internal self-discipline. In those circumstances where internal mechanisms fail, a new kind of juridical authority may be required.

7. Students rightly expect administrators to exercise leadership, to take the initiative in proposing educational changes suited to a changing clientele and a changing society. But just as students are entitled to acceptance of their rights and responsibilities, so are administrators. Students should recognize that the administrator is responsible to widely divergent campus groups and is accountable to the board which legally governs the institution. Within these limitations, he must have freedom to initiate, guide, negotiate, and make decisions, if the institution is not to remain static. Attempts to circumscribe this freedom will either reinforce the status quo or create chaos.

FACULTY

All the constituent groups share concern over the appropriate role of the faculty. Their chief criticism is that the professorial role—particularly in major universities—has become so distorted in the direction of research and scholarly achievement that many faculty seriously neglect their teaching function. That this is a real problem is substantiated by considerable evidence. In national surveys, for example, students complain repeatedly about lack of contact with faculty and faculty indifference to student needs. These complaints are especially common in major research-oriented universities. Studies comparing the environments of universities with those of smaller colleges reveal among the former a comparative lack of student and faculty interaction in the classroom, an impersonal relationship between teacher and students, and a feeling on the part of students that the institution lacks concern for their individual development. It is significant that the major universities have been the prime targets of violent and disruptive protest.

The research commitments that draw professors away from teaching are upheld in a variety of ways. One factor is the strong demand for research services from both government and business. Another is the prestige accruing to institutions that employ distinguished research scholars. Many institutions find the temptation of instant departmental prestige and large research grants and contracts to be irresistible. Since the research-oriented faculty tend to recruit, screen, and train their replacements, the system is self-perpetuating.

The imbalanced emphasis on research, away from teaching, is also supported by the lopsided competition between the institutions and the scholarly discipline for the loyalty and concern of faculty members. Both teaching and research figure among a faculty member's contributions to his institution (though formalized procedures for evaluating teaching are rare, and public evidence is far more readily available on research competence). So far as the faculty member's standing in his discipline is concerned, however, with only rare exceptions—such as the authorship of innovative textbooks—it is solely published research that counts. Published research is what establishes the scholar's prestige among his peers in other colleges and universities. In the university world, therefore, it is also the main source of his economic value in the academic marketplace. No ambitious young faculty member can afford to neglect his disciplinary standing as determined by his published research. His movement from one institution to another is heavily influenced by the time and support he will gain for his research efforts.

Of course, many research-oriented faculty in universities teach graduate students as part of their research activity. Indeed, in many fields of graduate study, the laboratory is the classroom. Prestigious professors who are not accessible to undergraduates may be very accessible to graduate students to whom they have their basic teaching responsibility. It is not the Committee's purpose to suggest that all professors dedicated entirely to research, or to research and graduate teaching, should now teach undergraduates. The problem lies with overemphasizing research at the expense of undergraduate teaching.

This Committee does not think it desirable, even were it possible, to devalue the contribution of scholarly research. Such research may, in fact, contribute to the solution of social ills about which students and others in the academic community are actively concerned. What deliberate policy can do is introduce compensating influences to redress the balance. Specific suggestions are put forth in the recommendations that follow.

1. Effective teaching deserves greater recognition in hiring, promoting, and paying, especially in the major in-

stitutions. Explicit methods must be developed for assessing teaching competence, improving the learning process, and systematically reviewing the adequacy of the curriculum. Quality of teaching must be given greater weight in tenure decisions. Faculty scholarship, research, and public service should relate more closely to teaching; indeed, they can enhance teaching. Both individual institutions and national professional organizations should establish fitting rewards for exceptional teachers. The Committee urges the learned and professional societies to explore other ways of giving more status to teaching and improving its quality, especially at the undergraduate level.

2. In matters affecting teaching—for example, new faculty appointments; the awarding of tenure; new courses, departments, or interdisciplinary arrangements—faculty committees should seek the counsel of students who have had direct experience with the matter to be decided. The faculty, by virtue of its earned competence, is in the best position to have main jurisdiction over academic matters. But students, as the consumers of higher education and as young people with important perceptions about our changing society, have a right to be heard on matters affecting the educational program. As was pointed out in an earlier recommendation, participation by students could strengthen the quality of the decisions made and help ensure their acceptability to the student body. In this connection, faculty should welcome the development by student organizations of formalized and objective procedures for evaluating faculty teaching of undergraduates in all important courses. Too often, student evaluations of teaching are fragmentary and are not available to the teacher, who might improve his teaching if he were aware of students' criticisms.

3. Tenure policies—concerning a faculty member's right to hold his academic appointment until retirement once competence has been demonstrated (except when extreme malfeasance has been established by due process)—need to be reappraised. The justification for tenure is the crucial protection it gives to academic freedom. Professors who espouse unpopular views must be free from reprisal. Tenure was not devised in the spirit of trade union systems to guarantee job security. But it has come to serve this function too, at a cost. It sometimes has been a shield for indifference and neglect of scholarly duties. At a time when an increasing number of teachers, especially in community colleges and state colleges, are organizing for collective bargaining, the Committee recognizes that a challenge to the present concept of tenure is no small matter, that the issues involved are complex and difficult to resolve, and that a satisfactory solution must maintain effective safeguards for academic freedom. Nonetheless, we urge the American Association of University Professors and the Association of American Colleges (co-sponsors of the basic 1940 Statement on Academic

Freedom and Tenure) to join with representatives of other educational organizations that are concerned with tenure, including the American Federation of Teachers, the United States National Student Association, and constituents of the American Council on Education, to reexamine existing policies. Standards for awarding tenure—a matter of institutional autonomy—need broadening to allow greater consideration of teaching ability. Scholarly communities must be protected as effectively as tenure now protects individual professors.

4. A climate of open discussion must be created in which risks for trying new approaches are minimized. Faculty members should respect the educational freedom of students in the classroom to raise questions and to discuss freely issues arising from their course work. To encourage innovations in curriculum, in degree requirements, and in standards for assessing faculty competence, institutions should seek resources to alter the reward system. Innovation can also be encouraged on our giant campuses through subdivisions with greatly dispersed authority, budgetary autonomy, and architectural settings that encourage informality and intimacy. In many institutions, the hierarchical structure of institutional management and departmental authority needs to be altered. Rigid hierarchies tend to shield the decision-makers from the discontents and constructive ideas of students and younger faculty members.

5. Renewed attention must be given to long-standing questions about the established standards for the Doctor of Philosophy degree. Either Ph.D. programs should be reformed to provide more adequately for the majority whose careers will in fact center on teaching rather than on the conduct of research, or increased recognition should be given to alternative programs for those who will be primarily teachers. One important issue is the nature of the dissertation. Generally the dissertation is supposed to be a work of original research, but this standard is not uniformly applied and is inappropriate for many graduate students. Another issue is the role of graduate students as teachers. Although some are excellent teachers, graduate students tend to pursue their teaching assignments without adequate supervision in a system which treats assistantships primarily as a form of subsidy to students and a source of low-cost instruction. Supervised experience in teaching, as well as participation in decisions on departmental policies, ought to be important parts of the learning experience, especially for those graduate students planning academic careers.

6. Faculty need to take a more active role in reexamining institutional goals and in guiding change, instead of simply responding to reform proposals from other quarters. Too often, in fact, their authority on educational matters has been used to disguise complacency and unwarranted conservatism,

and as an excuse to avoid making reforms. Many have resisted changes designed to meet the varied needs of a heterogeneous student body because they conceive their own role narrowly and selectively, as simply the trainers of an intellectual elite. Faculty need to reexamine critically both their role and their procedures for handling innovative ideas.

ADMINISTRATORS

It is altogether proper for the other constituent groups to hold administrators accountable for their actions and their inactions—but only within the limits of their roles and responsibilities and their power to act. When their responsibilities are ill-defined or their power to act is unduly circumscribed, serious barriers exist to the resolution of campus tensions.

1. Administrators are often properly blamed for their institution's shortcomings in organization and governance. Other members of the college community, however, are typically uncertain about what administrators are expected to do and how their performance should be evaluated. Accordingly, institutions must define explicitly who is responsible for what. Moreover, administrators often have responsibilities in certain areas but do not have the power to take major action without approval from higher authority or endorsement from a faculty committee. These limitations, too, should be clearly spelled out.

2. Especially at the presidential level, responsibility must be accompanied by the necessary authority. Trustees, faculty, and students need to consider the possible ultimate consequence to themselves of weakening the president's authority. Institutions should have constitutions or bylaws which clearly define the responsibility *and* the authority of the president. In this connection, the nature of the presidency deserves rethinking. For example, fixed terms of office, renewable or unrenewable, might relieve some pressures on presidents and also ensure institutional vitality. Fixed terms, or a system by which to review administrative tenure, might be preferable to the present system in which some presidents stay long beyond their real effectiveness or are sometimes sacrificed after one major incident. A division of authority—between "outside" concerns and "inside" ones, for example—might be considered where the burdens of the presidential office have grown too large for one man.

3. Colleges and universities also need to reassess the roles and responsibilities of other administrative officers. Their performance should be subjected to periodic review and evaluation. Additionally, the roles of administrative offices should be reexamined. For example, on some campuses the dean of students serves as adviser to students and overseer of student organizations, while also serving as prose-

cutor (and sometimes as judge and jury) in disciplinary matters. These responsibilities may conflict with one another and call for differing talents, and, where feasible, should be separated—the advisory responsibility assigned to one office, and judicatory responsibility to another.

4. Presidents and other administrators have an especially urgent responsibility to ensure that avenues of communication are open. Some presidents are cut off by over-conscientious aides or secretaries; others are seldom seen on campus and never talk with students and seldom with faculty. How to keep the channels open will present a different problem on every campus. Nevertheless, it should always be possible for a student, faculty member, trustee, or layman who has a message to get through to the president. Accessibility, moreover, is not the whole answer. Presidents and other administrators must take positive steps to explain their plans and policies to the appropriate constituencies, through such devices as newsletters, annual reports, "town meetings," or position papers on particular issues. They must also provide students, faculty, and others with information sufficiently in advance to enable them to make contributions to decisions.

5. To communicate effectively administrators must be open and candid in giving reasons for decisions and actions. There are instances when the release of information would needlessly injure individuals. But the withholding of information on such occasions will be better understood and accepted if, at all other times, communication is candid. Here, also, continuing efforts are as important as those during crisis. Administrators should meet frequently with faculty and student groups, not only to listen but also to make known their thinking on basic issues.

6. The ability of presidents and other administrative officers to devote the time required for the communications we consider desirable is dependent on adequate institutional staffing. Highly effective administrative organization, procedures, and personnel to conduct the heavy administrative business of the institution, are needed to support presidents and other administrators as they devote themselves to the varied and time-consuming responsibilities of modern institutional governance.

7. The rules by which colleges and universities govern themselves, and the defining of appropriate responses to infractions, are matters on which students, faculty, administrators, and trustees should seek agreement. But it is an administrative responsibility (if only by default) to see that these rules and procedures receive continuing assessment. Rules need to be tested for clarity, fairness, and adequacy to meet foreseeable circumstances. In many institutions administrators need to initiate a rulebook "housecleaning": to eliminate (or draw to the attention of those empowered to do so) rules that have outlived their usefulness, or are unrelated

to institutional objectives, or that duplicate public laws and carry unwarranted additional punishment.

8. Administrators need to develop with civil authorities, especially law enforcement agencies, plans for handling campus disturbances that would require the presence of civil authorities. The plans must define the division of responsibility between campus and civil authorities, provide effective channels of communication between the two groups, and ensure due restraint in the handling of those causing the disturbance. The entry of large numbers of off-campus police during disturbances can heighten tensions rather than relieve them. Physically punitive action, however provoked, that can be interpreted as "police brutality" adds fuel to the flames. Inaction, on the other hand, can result in substantial property damage, danger to members of the campus community, and extended interruption of educational function, as well as reduced respect for the administration.

TRUSTEES

As most informed critics of academic governance have concluded, the lay board, despite its shortcomings, is still preferable to other methods of control. The reform of board organization and procedures should be undertaken even though no mere redefinition of trustee roles will eliminate existing frictions. Failure to make lay boards more effective participants in the total enterprise, however, is certain to increase the tensions now disturbing much of higher education. The effectiveness of trustees is not measured by the depth of their involvement in the day-to-day business of the institution or the firmness of their control. It is measured, rather, by the extent to which they are well informed on educational issues, judicious in the exercise of their powers, and protective of the prerogatives of all members of the academic community.

1. Every institution should have carefully framed bylaws subject to periodic reexamination, that set forth the board's essential authority and responsibility and define its procedures. Periodic review of the bylaws will benefit from outside counsel and from attention to what other institutions are doing. Even such basic matters as the board's mode of selection and appointment, size, composition, term of office, should be reexamined. For example, switching to popular election of boards might dissuade men of detached viewpoint from applying, but self-perpetuating boards of lifetime members have faults as well. Institutions with the latter system should consider that fixed terms for trustees would preserve detachment and continuity, while at the same time ensuring periodic rejuvenation of the board.

2. Students, faculty, and others need to be well informed about how decisions are made in their institution and

the reasons for policies that are decided. The bylaws of the trustees should be accessible to all members of the academic community and to concerned outsiders, as should agenda of each meeting. When major decisions are made, boards should promptly issue reports which explain reasons for the actions taken. Boards must have well-publicized rules governing the submission of petitions and adequate procedures for their prompt consideration.

3. Boards should make more effective use of special committees and other mechanisms through which they and representatives of students, faculty, staff, and alumni can communicate more readily.

4. In the matter of finances, ways must be found to re-examine institutional priorities so that there will be both wider opportunity for involvement and a greater sharing of responsibility among students, faculty, staff, and others.

5. Delegation of responsibility and accountability does not absolve trustees of the need to be well informed about the institution's programs and to be serious students of higher education generally. Presidents and others who influence heavily the content of the board agenda should focus it more on educational issues and less on fiscal and house-keeping chores.

6. Although anything resembling a quota scheme of representation in board membership should be avoided, there should be greater diversity of age, occupation, and other salient individual characteristics that might broaden horizons and present other points of view. Some boards of trustees may wish to consider adding student and faculty members from their own institutions; other boards, desiring to avoid the possible conflicts of interests that may arise from such participation, can achieve broadened viewpoints by adding members drawn from other institutions. Ultimately, the evolving nature of higher education may require re-examination and reassessment of the authority and functions of trustees in the governance of the university, along with re-appraisal of a need to delegate some of their authority to other groups on the campus.

GENERAL RECOMMENDATIONS: GOVERNANCE

In certain basic areas of governance and decision making, many institutions have considerable autonomy to chart their own course. It is in these areas that the diverse interests of the members of the academic community are most likely to be reconciled. These include: (1) criteria for admissions; (2) criteria for recruiting, hiring, and promoting faculty and staff; (3) curriculum requirements; (4) performance standards and rewards for faculty and staff; (5) standards of conduct for members of the academic community; (6) academic performance standards for students, including criteria for grading and certification.

The Committee believes that campus conflict sometimes arises from a confusion of three questions: (1) the substance of a particular policy: What is it?; (2) its validity: Is it a good policy?; (3) the process by which it was made: Who decided it? To view campus tensions in terms simply of "Who decides?" rather than of "What gets decided?" is to regard institutional decision making as a power struggle rather than as a means of improving the educational environment. Validity is, of course, one important consideration, and educational decisions are most likely to be valid if alternatives have first been subjected to a complete airing and analysis by the parties concerned.

The need for thorough study of alternatives relates closely to the problem of communication. All four constituent groups cite inadequate communication as a major cause of tension. Decisions made without adequate study or simply presented as fait accompli not only create resentment and hostility, but also run the risk of being wrong. This is particularly true with decisions on strictly educational matters (curricular requirements, for example), where students, faculty, and others directly affected are likely to have valuable insights to contribute. Although improved communication does not eliminate problems, it usually results in sounder educational decisions and fosters governance by consensus rather than by force.

1. The processes of academic governance, especially those that determine and establish institutional policies, must be seen by all major groups concerned as essentially *fair*. Due process must be enlarged to include broad participation in the deliberations on important issues. If any part of the academic community feels that its own interest in a proposed new institutional policy has not been fairly presented and heard, the new policy is likely to be challenged.

2. Every attempt must be made to establish effective communications, so that policy questions and grievances can be aired by the campus community. A number of institutions have had success with such communications methods as (1) centralized files of important institutional records accessible to campus constituents; (2) rumor centers, especially during periods of campus turmoil, to which members of the community may telephone for accurate and up-to-date information; (3) ombudsmen to hear grievances, speed up communications, and unsnarl red tape; and (4) "official" campus newspapers, in which texts of important reports and other documents of wide interest to the campus community can appear. Members of the campus community should recognize that improved channels of consultation may render decision-making procedures slower and more cumbersome.

3. As an aid to effective decision making, joint administrative-faculty-student committees should be established, wherever possible, to assist in resolving the problem and attaining the objective. More institutions should experiment with permanent legislative assemblies composed of administrators, faculty, and students. Some issues are better dealt with by faculty assemblies, some by student groups, and some by the president and his administrative staff; but each group's decision-making processes can benefit from inputs from the other groups. There are, additionally, issues of concern to all three groups which should be dealt with by a governance system in which all are recognized as legitimate participants.

4. The effective functioning of a college or university depends in large measure upon a shared commitment by members of the campus community to the principle of institutional self-governance and an assumption of the responsibilities that such a commitment implies. For example, in disciplinary proceedings all must be willing to provide testimony and to serve as triers of fact. It must be possible to conduct hearings without fear of disruption or retaliation against participants; there must be willingness to respect the finality of decisions.

GENERAL RECOMMENDATIONS: INSTITUTIONAL GOALS

The Committee's recommendations rest on shared views about the appropriate roles of colleges and universities in an unstable and troubled world. The problems of colleges and universities, like those of society at large, rule out as untenable a comfortable policy of "business as usual." As society gropes to discover and realize more humane, just, and viable patterns of life in an age of advanced technology on a crowded globe, colleges and universities need to develop mechanisms of "self-renewal," in John Gardner's phrase, to keep them in position to make appropriate contributions to society. In their educational function, colleges and universities need renewal to enhance their ability to prepare young people to cope with the kind of world that they will actually encounter.

1. Everywhere there is need to reexamine existing disciplines and to allocate resources for the design of new forms of intellectual inquiry; interdisciplinary programs which break down departmental rigidity provide one example of an appropriate response.

2. Faculties and staff of colleges and universities should be drawn from more diverse social and vocational backgrounds. The vocational experiences of artists, writers, diplomats, government officials, and others can enrich and enliven the discourse on the campus and help to reduce the tendency toward academic provincialism.

3. Colleges and universities must respond, more effectively than they have in the past, to the educational desires of women. Wherever discrimination because of sex exists, it must be eliminated.

4. New curricula and resources are needed to further the self-development of students in ways traditional curricula have failed to do. More institutions should seek the resources to experiment with alternate modes of learning: cluster colleges, experiential education, work-study, community involvement for academic credit, and other living-learning arrangements.

5. Institutions should create centers for educational research and innovation to encourage the development of new approaches to education, to encourage the implementation of innovation in education—both in teaching techniques and in new courses, and to foster a continual questioning of conventional and traditional means of promoting the expansion of our frontiers of knowledge.

6. The American society overemphasizes the value of the traditional college degree. Further encouragement should be given to the development and support of new directions in postsecondary education.

7. Novel admissions practices should be tried by some institutions, both to extend access to higher education and to provide a broader population in which to test the quality and effectiveness of education programs.

8. Most collegiate institutions in the past have been heavily oriented to the purposes of the white majority. More attention must be given to the needs of ethnic minorities. Ethnic studies programs, however, should ultimately be incorporated into the regular academic programs so that the white majority will learn more about the history and needs of minority groups.

9. Institutions should recruit more students, faculty, and staff from minority groups that have been underrepresented in the campus population. Other institutions should not be "raided" for minority personnel and students; rather, though it will take time, the pool of eligibles must be enlarged and recruitments made from among those who would not normally expect to attend college or to have academic careers.

10. Many reforms in higher education are expensive. But if we are to have them, institutions must be given greatly increased funding from all sources—especially the federal government—to increase financial aid to students, to develop new kinds of educational programs, and to permit students as well as faculty to launch innovative research and teaching projects.

11. Trustees, administrators, and faculty have as great a stake in effecting institutional change as do students. Reform of the college is a shared responsibility requiring attitudes that encourage educational change by all of the campus constituents.

12. Institutions should resist the distortion of their research efforts because of outside sources of funds. We urge the federal government to support research and instruction in ways that will respect the autonomy of institutions, enhance scholarly innovation, and improve students' educational opportunities, and we also urge institutions to emphasize these principles in developing their research.

CONCLUSION

UNREST on the nation's campuses is only part of the mosaic of problems in American society: the poverty amid affluence, the continuing racial strife, the poisoned environment, the decaying cities, the apparent decline in the whole quality of life. These problems affect all of society, not simply colleges and universities. It is ironic that some seek destruction of the colleges and universities and that others within them remain averse to all constructive change.

These institutions hold our greatest hopes: as places of objective inquiry, for the solutions of society's problems; places of unfettered thought, for the debate of sensitive issues without fear of intimidation or reprisal; centers of teaching and learning, for the education of tomorrow's problem-solvers and leaders.

Just as those who compose the academic community must rise to the defense of colleges and universities as vital and enduring social institutions, so must they recognize that these institutions must be responsive to the needs of the times. A college or university should be flexible enough to accommodate change, aggressive enough to promote change, and wise enough to anticipate the consequences of change. It must strive as never before to become a bastion of high purpose, a goad to the public conscience, an implacable enemy of the false, the inhumane, and the unjust. And in doing so, it must defend the use of reason as the means of moving toward its own and society's goals.

The survival of our system of higher education and its long-term contribution to society depend upon rationality and civility, shared concern, and mutual respect among the members of the academic community. Students, faculty, administrators, trustees—all must recognize their necessary interdependence.

NOTES

1. For a list of consultants, see Appendix A.

2. Statistical evidence presented here, and in chap. 1, is drawn from recent research findings of the American Council on Education, especially from Alan E. Bayer and Alexander W. Astin, "Violence and Disruption on the U.S. Campus, 1968–69," *Educational Record,* Fall 1969. The authors defined violent protest as any campus incident which involved (a) burning of a building; (b) damage to a building or furnishings; (c) destruction of files, records, or papers; (d) campus march, picketing, or rally with physical violence; and (e) the injury or death of any person. Nonviolent disruptive protest was defined as any campus incident which involved (a) occupation of a building; (b) barring of entrance to a building; (c) holding officials captive; (d) interruption of classes, speeches, or meetings; and (e) general campus strike or boycott of classes or school functions. The characterizations are those of Bayer and Astin, *not* of this Committee.

3. New York: Basic Books, 1968.

4. Bettelheim, "Obsolete Youth," *Encounter,* September 1969, pp. 29–42.

5. *To Establish Justice, To Insure Domestic Tranquility: Final Report of the National Commission on the Causes and Prevention of Violence* (Washington: Government Printing Office, 1969), p. 211.

6. *Final Report,* pp. 210–11.

7. Robert F. Boruch, *The Faculty Role in Campus Unrest,* ACE Research Reports, Vol. 4, No. 5, 1969.

8. Martin Trow, "Reflections on the Transition from Mass to Universal Higher Education," *Daedalus,* Winter 1970, pp. 41–42, n. 16.

9. George Duke Humphrey, "Securing Legislative Appropriations: An Administrative Viewpoint," in Association of Governing Boards of State Universities and Allied Institutions, *Proceedings,* 1949.

10. Student rights and guidelines for disciplinary proceedings are discussed in the report of the American Bar Association's Commission on Campus Government and Student Dissent. See also "Joint Statement on Rights and Freedoms of Students," *AAUP Bulletin,* Summer 1968.

APPENDIX A

Consultants and Authors of Background Papers

BENNETT M. BERGER
Professor of Sociology, University of California, Davis
WILLIAM M. BIRENBAUM
President, Staten Island Community College
LANDRUM R. BOLLING
President, Earlham College
KENNETH E. BOULDING
Professor of Economics, University of Colorado
SANDY CHADWICK
Student, American University
ALLEN CLOUD
Student, Grinnell College
NORMAN COUSINS
Editor, *Saturday Review*
CARL DAVIDSON
Assistant Editor, *The Guardian*
THOMAS C. DAWSON
Editor, *Stanford Daily,* Stanford University
DOUGLAS F. DOWD
Professor of Economics, Cornell University
DUANE DRAPER
President, Association of Student Governments
JACK EDENS
Association of Student Governments
DAVID A. HENDERSON
Campus Affairs Vice-President
United States National Student Association
RALPH HETZEL
Trustee, Pennsylvania State University
ROBERT M. HUNDLEY
Student, Columbia University
JUDSON JEROME
Director, Center for Documentary Arts, Antioch Columbia
(Antioch College at Columbia, Maryland)
DAVID JOHNSON
Association of Student Governments
LOUIS JOUGHIN
Associate Secretary, American Association
of University Professors

JOSEPH F. KAUFFMAN
President, Rhode Island College

DAVID A. KEENE
National Chairman, Young Americans for Freedom

KENNETH KENISTON
Professor of Psychology, School of Medicine
Yale University

CLARK KERR
Chairman, Carnegie Commission on Higher Education

DAVID J. LANGSTON
Student, Columbia University

SEYMOUR MARTIN LIPSET
Professor of Government and Social Relations
Harvard University

DEAN E. McHENRY
Chancellor, University of California, Santa Cruz

STEVEN MULLER
Vice-President for Public Affairs, Cornell University

JOHN A. PEOPLES, JR.
President, Jackson State College

RICHARD E. PETERSON
Research Psychologist, Educational Testing Service

SAMUEL D. PROCTOR
Professor, Graduate School of Education
Rutgers University

ROGER RAPOPORT
Former Editor, *The Michigan Daily*
University of Michigan

MARCUS RASKIN
Co-Director, Institute for Policy Studies
Trustee, Antioch College

MORTON A. RAUH
Vice-President, Antioch College

WILLIAM M. ROTH
Trustee, University of California

PETER SCHRAG
Editor, *Change*

EDWARD SCHWARTZ
Former President, United States National
Student Association

CHARLES E. SHEPARD
Student, Northwestern University

ANDREW SIDELL
Student Body President, Pratt Institute of Technology

CHARLES SUTTON
Association of Student Governments

IAN M. THOMPSON
Durango, Colorado

STEVEN J. TONSOR
Associate Professor of History, University of Michigan

DAVID WANSER
Association of Student Governments

HARRIS L. WOFFORD, JR.
President, State University of New York College
at Old Westbury

GWENDOLYN PATTON WOODS
National Coordinator
National Association of Black Students

E. WILLIAM ZIEBARTH
Dean, College of Liberal Arts, University of Minnesota
Trustee, Macalester College

J. L. ZWINGLE
Executive Vice-President, Association
of Governing Boards of Universities and Colleges

Statistical Tables on Campus Unrest, 1968-69

Table 1: Protest Issues at Institutions Experiencing Incidents of Violent or Nonviolent Disruptive Protest: 1968–1969 Academic Year

Weighted Population Estimates

Protest Issue	Among Institutions Experiencing Violent Protests (N = 145)		Among Institutions Experiencing Nonviolent Disruptive Protests (N = 379)	
	N	Percent	N	Percent
1. U.S. military policy (e.g., Vietnam, CBW, ABM)...........	56	38.6	144	38.0
2. Selective service policy.............................	40	27.6	88	23.2
3. ROTC programs......................................	55	37.9	65	17.1
4. On-campus military or government research.............	43	29.6	40	10.6
5. On-campus recruiting by government or industry.........	52	35.9	114	30.1
Total, war-related issues (1-5)............................	71	49.0	194	51.2
6. Institutional services (e.g., food and medical services, housing and recreation facilities)......................	45	31.0	105	27.7
7. Institutional parietal rules (e.g., dress, dormitory regulations, drinking, sex, required attendance at school functions)...	20	13.8	136	35.9
8. Institutional student disciplinary practices..............	67	46.2	102	26.9
9. Instructional procedures (e.g., class size, quality of instruction, grading system, student evaluation)...........	36	24.8	125	33.0
10. Tuition charges and fees.............................	17	11.7	36	9.5
Total, services to students issues (6, 9, 10).................	64	44.1	193	50.9
11. Special educational programs for minority groups (e.g., black studies, compensatory programs).................	96	66.2	194	51.2
12. Special admissions policies for minority groups..........	55	37.9	97	25.6
Total, minority group students issues (11-12)................	101	69.1	196	51.7
13. Civil rights (e.g., desegregation, voter registration).......	7	4.8	17	4.5
14. Labor problems (e.g., wages, benefits, unionization)......	28	19.3	10	2.6
15. Administrative indifference or inaction concerning local community problems...............................	61	42.1	29	7.6
Total, off-campus issues (1-5; 13-15)......................	102	70.3	214	56.5
16. Police brutality......................................	37	25.5	13	3.4
17. Requests or demands for amnesty......................	46	31.7	50	13.2
18. Administrative indifference or inaction concerning previous protest grievances.............................	63	43.4	106	28.0
19. Administrative response to previous protests............	45	31.0	67	17.7
20. Mourning for students or others killed or wounded.......	22	15.2	34	9.0
Total, secondary issues (16-20)...........................	96	66.2	157	41.4
21. Student participation in decision making (e.g., inclusion on committees)......................................	78	53.8	147	38.8
22. Free expression (e.g., censorship of publications, exclusion of "controversial" speakers)......................	19	13.1	51	13.5
23. Faculty (e.g., academic freedom, hiring, tenure)..........	51	35.2	65	17.1
Total, student power issues (7, 8, 21-23)....................	113	77.9	283	74.7
24. Other..	30	20.7	60	15.8
Grand total (1-24).......................................	145	100.0	379	100.0

Source: Tables 1-5 are from "Violence and Disruption on the U.S. Campus, 1968-69," Educational Record, *Fall 1969.*

Table 2: Immediate Outcomes of Protest Incidents on Campuses Experiencing
Violent or Nonviolent Disruptive Protest: 1968–1969 Academic Year

Weighted Population Estimates

Direct Results and Consequences	Among 145 Institutions Experiencing Violent Protests		Among 379 Institutions Experiencing Nonviolent Disruptive Protests	
	N	Percent	N	Percent
1. National Guard called in	2	1.4	0	0.0
2. Off-campus police called in	80	55.2	45	11.9
3. One or more persons killed	8	5.5	0	0.0
4. Some persons injured	45	31.0	0	0.0
5. Some protesters arrested	82	56.6	19	5.0
6. Some protesters indicted	37	25.5	10	2.6
Total, civil action against individual students (5-6)	87	60.0	24	6.3
7. Temporary restraining order or court injunction obtained	28	19.3	25	6.6
8. Classes suspended	60	41.4	42	11.1
9. National press or television coverage given to protest	69	47.6	143	37.7
10. Administration or faculty negotiated issues with demonstrators	90	62.1	316	83.4
11. Formal statement issued by faculty in support of protesters	43	29.6	67	17.7
12. One or more students dismissed or expelled	21	14.5	19	5.0
13. Some students suspended or put on probation	48	33.1	69	18.2
14. Formal student reprimands issued	52	35.8	41	10.8
15. Financial assistance withdrawn from some protesters	13	9.0	6	1.6
Total, major institutional discipline against individual students (12, 13, 15)	56	38.6	80	21.1
Total, either civil or institutional action against individual students (5, 6, 12, 13, 15)	109	75.2	84	22.2
16. Some faculty or administrators resigned as a result of the protest	13	9.0	2	0.5
17. Other	23	15.9	29	7.6

Table 3: Institutional Changes as Related to Major Incidents of Campus Protest, 1968–1969 Academic Year

Weighted Population Estimates

Changes	As a Direct Result of Protest Incident				Not as a Direct Result of Protest Incident					
	On Campuses Experiencing Violent Protests		On Campuses Experiencing Nonviolent Disruptive Protests		On Campuses Experiencing Violent Protests		On Campuses Experiencing Nonviolent Disruptive Protests		On Campuses Not Experiencing Violent or Nonviolent Disruptive Protests	
	(N=145)		(N=379)		(N=145)		(N=379)		(N=1818)	
	N	Percent	N	Percent	N	Percent	N	Percent	N	Percent
1. Establishment of black studies program or department..........	68	46.9	34	9.0	44	30.3	186	49.1	324	17.8
2. Institution of other curriculum changes......................	32	22.1	74	19.5	86	59.3	218	57.5	749	41.2
3. Institution of special admissions policies for minority group members.....................	23	15.9	19	5.0	38	26.2	76	20.1	155	8.5
Total, changes in racial policies (1, 3).	80	55.2	42	11.1	61	42.1	202	53.3	424	23.3
4. Liberalization of parietal rules....	8	5.5	47	12.4	78	53.8	156	41.2	448	24.6
5. Changes in institutional rules and regulations governing students...	17	11.7	54	14.2	79	54.5	187	49.3	746	41.0
6. Provision to students of greater voice or representation on existing committees...................	33	22.8	69	18.2	81	55.9	194	51.2	823	45.3
Total, changes in student power (4-6).	37	25.5	118	31.1	104	71.7	258	68.1	1,062	58.4
7. Formation of new committees or study groups on campus.........	78	53.8	131	34.6	89	61.4	145	38.3	604	33.2
8. Termination of ROTC program....	4	2.8	2	0.5	0	0.0	0	0.0	3	0.2
9. Changes in ROTC program, such as making it elective............	16	11.0	14	3.7	4	2.8	16	4.2	19	1.0
10. Discontinuation of some campus research for the military.........	0	0.0	0	0.0	2	1.4	2	0.5	0	0.0
11. Prohibition of on-campus recruiting for some organizations.......	6	4.1	12	3.2	0	0.0	0	0.0	11	0.6
Total, substantive institutional changes (1-6, 8-11)..................	104	71.7	204	53.8	116	80.0	336	88.6	1,128	62.0
12. Other........................	13	9.0	31	8.2	5	3.4	5	1.3	36	2.0

Table 4: Institutional Size and Incidence of Violent and Nonviolent Disruptive Protest by Type of Institution

Weighted Population Estimates

Enrollment	Two-Year Colleges			Four-Year Colleges			Universities		
	N	Percent with Violent Protest	Percent with Nonviolent Disruptive Protest	N	Percent with Violent Protest	Percent with Nonviolent Disruptive Protest	N	Percent with Violent Protest	Percent with Nonviolent Disruptive Protest
Under 500...............	224	0.0	0.0	129	3.1	4.7	54	0.0	0.0
500–999................	169	0.0	0.0	394	2.5	17.5			
1,000–5,000.............	303	4.3	2.6	591	5.4	23.5	29	13.8	69.0
Over 5,000.............	68	16.2	35.3	159	13.8	23.9	222	22.1	42.0
Total...............	764	3.1	4.2	1,273	5.3	19.8	305	17.4	31.1

Table 5: Institutional Selectivity and Incidence of Violent and Nonviolent Disruptive Protest by Type of Institution

Weighted Population Estimates

Selectivity Level	Two-Year Colleges			Four-Year Colleges			Universities		
	N	Percent with Violent Protest	Percent with Nonviolent Disruptive Protest	N	Percent with Violent Protest	Percent with Nonviolent Disruptive Protest	N	Percent with Violent Protest	Percent with Nonviolent Disruptive Protest
Low....................	608	3.0	5.2	307	3.9	14.0	72	0.0	0.0
Low intermediate........	150	4.0	0.0	362	5.2	7.0	51	11.8	5.8
High intermediate........	6	0.0	0.0	454	4.2	28.2	124	19.4	53.2
High...................				150	12.0	37.3	58	39.7	44.8
Total...............	764	3.1	4.2	1,273	5.3	19.8	305	17.4	31.1

Note: The institutional selectivity score is the median standardized score on the ACT, SAT, or National Merit Scholarship Qualifying Test for students entering each U.S. college or university. These scores are coded into seven broad categories of institutional selectivity. For further specification of data sources and procedures, see Alexander W. Astin, *Predicting Success in College* (New York: Free Press, forthcoming).